THE NEGROES ARE CONGREGATING

THE NEGROES ARE CONGREGATING

BY NATASHA ADIYANA MORRIS

PLAYWRIGHTS CANADA PRESS
TORONTO

LIBRARY AND ARCHIVES CANADA CATALOGUING IN PUBLICATION
Title: The negroes are congregating / Natasha Adiyana Morris.
Names: Adiyana Morris, Natasha, author.
Description: A collection of drama scenes.
Identifiers: Canadiana (print) 20220432457 | Canadiana (ebook) 20220432511 | ISBN 9780369103918 (softcover) | ISBN 9780369103925 (EPUB) | ISBN 9780369103932 (PDF)
Classification: LCC PS8601.D5285 N44 2022 | DDC C812/.6—DC23

Playwrights Canada Press operates on land which is the ancestral home of the Anishinaabe Nations (Ojibwe / Chippewa, Odawa, Potawatomi, Algonquin, Saulteaux, Nipissing, and Mississauga), the Wendat, and the members of the Haudenosaunee Confederacy (Mohawk, Oneida, Onondaga, Cayuga, Seneca, and Tuscarora), as well as Metis and Inuit peoples. It always was and always will be Indigenous land.

We acknowledge the support of the Canada Council for the Arts, the Ontario Arts Council (OAC), Ontario Creates, and the Government of Canada for our publishing activities.

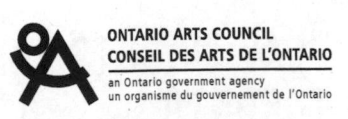

For Grandma "Pearly"

Tea with condensed milk, mackerel 'n fried dumpling, Sunday service, a bed made of endless woven sheets, and nuff love.

The Negroes Are Congregating was first workshopped at the PIECE OF MINE Festival in 2016. After excellent audience reaction, the play was further developed and presented through the following companies and at the following festivals: Black Theatre Network's 32nd Annual Conference in Memphis, Tennessee, July 2018; Toronto's SummerWorks Performance Festival, August 2018; Halifax Fringe, September 2018; the Atlanta Black Theatre Festival, October 2018 and April 2019; Théâtre de l'Usine in Geneva, Switzerland, January 2019; and the DC Black Theatre & Arts Festival in Washington, DC, July 2019. All above presentations were directed by Natasha Adiyana Morris and performed by Angaer Arop, David Delisca, and Dennis W. Langley.

The play was produced again by PIECE OF MINE Arts with the support of Theatre Passe Muraille, at Theatre Passe Muraille, Toronto, from February 29 to March 14, 2020, with the following cast and creative team:

Performed by Uche Ama, Christopher Bautista, and Christopher Parker

Written and Directed by Natasha Adiyana Morris
Produced and Production Managed by Troy Defour
Dramaturgy by Donna-Michelle St. Bernard
and Lincoln Anthony Blades
Stage Management by Christie Maingot
Production Design/Wardrobe Design by Nalo Soyini Bruce
Lighting Design by Lance Brathwaite
Assistant Production Design/Wardrobe Design by Krystin Leigh Smith
Production Assistance by Tinesha Richards

PLAYWRIGHT'S NOTES

This play poses a question: What is Black liberation? The pillaging of Africa(ns) is deep-rooted and widespread. It doesn't start with slavery nor end with Obama. But there are answers in the blood and that's what this play draws from. Each character brings their own essence to this question. It's never quite answered, I don't think it can be. I believe it is important to include many different perspectives and lived experiences that centre this founding question, for both the audience and creative team. Still, the play is biased towards a West Indian working class culture that I was raised in and does not encompass the endless fabrics of diverse African/African diasporic communities that exist in Canada.

Themes of physical, mental, and spiritual freedom cycle from beginning to end. There is no fourth wall.

Each performance is intended to be followed by an audience discussion, meant to allow people to openly dialogue amongst each other about the themes/scenes, rather than a Q&A with the creative team.

ROLES

There are three performers, all of African descent/Black. Each performer is assigned a character per scene unless stated otherwise, such as ENSEMBLE. The director will assign the performers as they see fit.

CHARACTERS IN ORDER OF APPEARANCE

Pastor (reccurring)
Black Twitter (reccurring)
Supporters 1 & 2
Audacity
Bishop
Cash
Winnie (reccurring)
MVP
Future
Preston (reccurring)
Ms. Henny
Latrell
Host
West Indian Ensemble
No Disrespek (reccurring)
Peter Bridlepath (reccurring)
Derrick Harper
Hotep Jigga
Angela (reccurring)
Fitzroy
Frederick Douglass
Old Head
Real Talk

Witness / 23
White Cop / Black Cop
Sticks N Stones
Sistren
Bredrin

SETTING

We are in the house of the Lord. Church. The audience should be configured to represent a faith-based sanctuary, pews are ideal, even if it is just the first row. Displayed at a focal point of the set is an image of Black Jesus or an African symbol, such as a Coptic cross or Sankofa, easily visible to the audience. Ideally, the image and/or symbol represents the African roots of the community in which the play is being performed.

INTERLUDE

This text is intended as a soundscape with scriptures overlapping.

i

am

that

i

am

And God saw everything that He had made,

Forgive us our trespasses

and, behold, it was very good.

—as we forgive those who trespass against us—

For what shall it profit a man

You were bought for a price

if he shall gain the whole world,

Don't become anyone's slave

Lose his own soul

Lose his own soul

The heart is deceitful

For His anger endureth but a moment

Desperately wicked

in His favour is life

I form the light, and create darkness:

He is not the God of the dead,

I make peace, and create evil:

but the God of the living

I the LORD do all these things

For ever and ever

Go and sin no more.

SCENE 1

Notes of gospel music fill the space as the audience settles in. Sunlight slowly comes up on stage setting the tone for service to begin. PASTOR *enters the space and walks to the pulpit, greeting the congregation along the way.*

Option to have lyrics projected for the audience to read/sing along with, as is the custom at many churches.

PASTOR *is dressed in a long robe of natural fabric, such as cotton or linen, with an African print scarf, such as kente cloth.*

The sermon following the gospel song is broken up into three parts over the course of the play, each intended to continue right where the last ended.

PASTOR

Opening song, sung a cappella.

How long was I wandering
On my own?
How far did I get,
Doing it alone?
Oh, God, I fell into a pit
Thinking it was home

And you pulled me out,
Yes, your mercy pulled me out

Verse one, with sound/music.

Purified.
Born again in spirit, I feel so alive
(ENSEMBLE) Mystified
For every tear swallowed, I swam out my pride
(ENSEMBLE) Amplified
When judgment day descends, there's nowhere to hide
(ENSEMBLE) Qualified
The first will be last and the last first in line.

Vocals intensify.

Verse two.

(ENSEMBLE) Sanctified
From before I was formed, to the day I die
(ENSEMBLE) Multiplied
Two fish and five loaves, my saviour wined and dined
(ENSEMBLE) Glorified
Through the shadow of death, your light is my guide
(ENSEMBLE) Sacrifice
My soul was saved through the blood of Christ

*PASTOR ad libs in between the final lyrics
sung by ENSEMBLE, such as "Oh, I feel the
Lord's presence" or "I need someone in
here to give God praise for qualifying you
when no one else saw your potential."*

Bridge.

ENSEMBLE
Purified
Mystified
Amplified
Qualified
Sanctified
Multiplied
Glorified
Sacrifice

PASTOR
My soul was saved through the blood of Christ

End of song.

God be the glory. Amen. Amen? Church, do you know how I measure my effectiveness as a leader—the length of time you all stay seated. The Lord calls us to exercise our precious but short life on earth, to put thoughts into words and words into action—otherwise we become spiritually lame. Weak, paralyzed, unable to move. I want us to turn to John 5:1-16. *(waits a moment for congregation to find passage)* Jesus came across a lame man at a pool in Jerusalem who surrounded himself among a multitude of sick people—every day—for thirty-eight years. The reason these unwell people congregated around the pool was because every so often an angel would come by and trouble the water, and whosoever went in first after the angel was healed from their infirmity.

Jesus asked the lame man if he wanted to be whole and he said he didn't have anyone to put him into the pool, that when he tried on his own, someone always got ahead. And what did Jesus tell him? "Stand up, pick up your mat, and walk!" And the man who had been lame for thirty-eight years was instantly healed.

Often, we're too afraid to fail in front of others so we expect those, who are willing and able, to carry us, and if they don't then we blame them for getting ahead. It's not enough to just stand up— you have to disrupt what you've become accustomed to. That's why he was instructed to pick up his mat, so as not to return to the place where the sick people amassed. And finally, walk. It turns out, he didn't need the water to be healed after all.

Blackout.

SCENE 2

BLACK TWITTER represents the new generation of Black thought on social media. It's pointed, satirical, and, usually, random AF.

BLACK TWITTER
The scariest shit I've ever seen is watching grown ppl swim in Lake Ontario. #fixitjesus

SCENE 3

We are in a public courtroom where a
civil-rights revolutionary, AUDACITY, *is*
on trial.
He has been imprisoned for over a year
because of the inability to afford an
exorbitant bail.

AUDACITY *slowly enters with handcuffs,*
moving with a defeated demeanour. Upon
hearing the applause from his supporters,
he is overwhelmed by their loyalty.

SUPPORTERS 1 & 2

Clapping and cheers of encouragement overlap.

Your name!?
Tell them your name brother!
C'mon now!
You're almost at the finish line!
Don't quit now!
What's your name?
Let them know.
Tell them your name!

AUDACITY

Chuckles and takes a moment to gather himself.

My name? Audacity.

I've got the most dangerous position in the world
A leader of Negroes. No way to be discreet about insubordination
When I arrive on site, those who weren't listening, subscribe to my every move
When I speak, I mess with a whole lotta people's money
When I make commands, I make enemies
I've been offered a few government jobs, a few plea deals, a dozen white women
White women love this kinky shit, bondage

> *Shakes handcuffs.*

But like Malcom X said, "If you don't stand for something, you'll fall for anything"

SUPPORTERS 1 & 2
/ "you'll fall for anything"

AUDACITY
Won't bow, so they hold me down
Politicians, judges, journalists with grudges
White, Black, and Black-whites
You know, house Negroes that might be light but not too bright

A Black prime minister won't keep me quiet
No, I think it's due time for another Yonge Street riot
That's what the headlines will call it
Even after they lock me up, for the setback
For being unapologetically BLACK
Acquittal.
Dismissal.
Our odds are looking pretty dismal, huh?

Where's the white saviour at?
The abolitionist that's going to lay down their life for my freedom?
Isn't that how we got emancipated?

> *SUPPORTER 1 uses a key to unlock*
> *AUDACITY from his handcuffs.*

AUDACITY
Harriet Tubman said—

SUPPORTER 1
No

SUPPORTER 2
Viola Desmond said—

SUPPORTER 1
No .

AUDACITY
Rosa Parks said—

SUPPORTER 1
Nah.

We good.
In between a rock and a hard place
Ripped and shipped away from everything that was us
Culture
Language
Inheritance
Identity

Portugal, Spain, Britain, France, Germany,
Belgium, Australia, America, Canada, Italy

It's not just a board game, Monopoly
Pirates after Africa, who can collect the most property?

> USHERS (*male performers*) *bring collection*
> *baskets through the audience.*

Collect the most interest from payday loan advances
Collect the most foreclosures from market avalanches
Collect the poorest youth, send them directly to jail
Assemble a new workforce, prisoners for sale

And finally, when we fight off every colonizer for our emancipation
In comes World Bank to shut down the celebration

> *A rapid sequence of disruption occurs.*
> *Money stained with blood falls from the*
> *ceiling and the performers enact chaos,*
> *grabbing the cash in a frantic manner,*
> *fueling a civil riot.* BISHOP *emerges as the*
> *chaos simmers, addressing his oppressors.*

BISHOP
You can't dead us
We know you're fed up
Black Twitter, SHOTS fired
The revolution it ah transpiah
Who you know, who you know?
Uncle Tom's resigning from Jim Crow
Who you know, who you know?

Colonies turned to enemies
It's getting harder to collect that dough
Lightskin pickaninnies don't call you daddy no mo'

We know God ain't got no colour
But if He did . . .
You know Obama played it safe
But if he didn't . . .
Who you know, who you know?
Who knows you?
Wake up in cold sweat
Who consoles you?
Money insulates that castle
But money is highly flammable too
What could you do when we
Huff and puff
And blow that house down?

> *Blows.*

Haaaaa!
Fuck your cracker house
I'm building an impenetrable empire
I'm just gon' need that oil, diamonds, gold, platinum, silver,
copper, iron, titanium, aluminum, uranium, cobalt, tantalum back.
Did you get that?
ASAP, ASAP

> *BISHOP's last line ("A.S.A.P.") and CASH's
> first line ("Negro, PLEEEASE") overlap.*

A.S.A.P. /

CASH

/ Negro, PLEEEASE
Shut the fuck up with that shit, bro

Everybody's not on this Black power, no shower tip
This is the hand I was dealt and I still make a grip
Move in silence, that's how you make 'em sick

Instead of getting your bread up, you're out here tempting the feds
And the moment they arrest you for being an heediot
You wanna bawl fi dead

And who got your bail money?
Your poor mother, still cleaning hospital beds

Where's the media whoring gotten you so far?
Do you have a house, a gyal, or even a car?

Not like you're changing anything that will actually last
Far as I'm concerned, we've got purple Desmonds
But in our community, the Black dollar doesn't last

And you know what really kills me, at the end of the day?
You cozy up to all dem white folks
Giving you play

How else is your false arrest breaking news
It's not real sympathy my nigga, they getting millions of views
They get the advertising money while you stay confused
But keep doing you, cause it sure ain't helping me
Chasing after oppression while begging to be free

*CASH walks off, grabs two brooms and
tosses one to BISHOP.
They both begin to sweep away the money
to the corners of the stage.*

SCENE 4

*We are transported to South Africa.
It is 1993 and* WINNIE MADIKIZELA-
MANDELA *(fifty-seven) is addressing
the country in her first presidential bid,
running against Nelson Mandela. This is a
fictional speech that reimagines a different outcome for South Africa's future,
post-apartheid. It addresses the process
in which apartheid-related crimes were
governed through the (factual) Truth and
Reconciliation Commission that took
place from December 1995–1998.* WINNIE
*is sharp, witty, and a natural public
speaker. The speech is broken up into three
parts over the course of the play that are
intended to continue right where the last
ended.*

WINNIE

Many believe I love to fight, that I wake up and say, "Please Lord,
grant me my daily bread and an extra serving of combat on the
side." No, no, no. I have had enough beatings from this outgoing
government and media to last me ten lifetimes. But what I can say
is, I am a woman who is not afraid to fight, and, if I decide to fight,
I fight to win.

I come before my people to run for president of South Africa, to
establish a political party that serves and protects the freedom
of our people, our right to be sovereign. The populous direc-
tion in which my former husband has chosen to lead is his own

undertaking, but I know that his plan will eventually steer us backwards and let our bloodshed be in vain. I have experienced and witnessed far too much cruelty to accept a mere game of "Never Have I Ever."

The leaked decision of Mr. Mandela to enact a Truth and Reconciliation Commission, as one of the first orders of business, is the common, grave mistake of our people. We are in a self-sabotaging habit of coddling our enemy. Rather than stand our ground to Afrikaners, who may pout and cry for the consequences they deserve, we are quick to forgive and absent-mindedly forget.

But consider how the white man has treated his own. Many Nazi war criminals swiftly committed suicide rather than face trial for their crimes, and those who were caught were hanged or imprisoned. And here we are, with a leader who is willing to provide amnesty . . . AMNESTY for a simple confession. Eish! Not even a slap on the wrist.

SCENE 5

We listen to an unconventional com-
mencement speech, in which MVP
rejects the label of being the "first Black"
attached to his accomplishment. He
proudly lays claim to his African heritage,
above an assigned colour.

MVP
I am not Black
I am African
I am not dark
This be melanin
I am brown-brown
Brown stew, brown view
Bronze chin, gold win
In sunshine I ripen

I am not a "POC"
Person of colour
I am not at-risk
In need of a collar
Dash wey minority, visibly or other
Naming me like a dog breed
On some *National Geographic* zoology

Don't need a next label
Like the ones from the past
Nigger, Negro, Coloured
Let Black be the last

I will sit where I see fit
Don't need a booster seat at thee table
Don't need to climb a ladder that's unstable
I ain't worried about getting blacker
I got juice to lend
I am not for sale during February
(laughs) Let's not pretend
I am not marching to prove that I matter
I am not sharing viral footage of us splattered
I am not a representation of my race
I am not hurting myself to take up space
I don't need a swab to reveal my DNA
I am not, I repeat NOT a descendent of slaves
I was made in the image of God. Okay.
I am that I am that I am that I am
Holy.
A little shea butter cleaness
A lotta royalty-hood-genius

I may not know my roots, but I know Western design
Box me into social housing without batting an eye
From Malvern to Tandridge to Oakwood & Vaughan
Suspensions, carding, and raids before dawn
Still, they can't keep a good man down
Who God bless will wear the crown
Swapping thorns for a black cap and gown
Bet. You'd never thought in a million years
Adversity. I still walk 'cross the stage of Queen's University

Throws graduation cap up in the air.

SCENE 6

BLACK TWITTER
You know the best thing white people invented? Ketchup.
Straight up.

> *As* BLACK TWITTER *begins to exit, a sub-tweet pops up that is visible to the audience and/or read aloud by* BLACK TWITTER.

SUBTWEET
Actually, ketchup dates back to Imperial China as a fermented fish sauce that did not consist of tomatoes. The Brits attempted to replicate the recipe and here we are.

BLACK TWITTER
Word. I tried yt ppl. I tried.

SCENE 7

A fable case study of urban economics.
FUTURE and PRESTON are two sides of the
same coin, venting about the challenges of
working alongside your people.

MS. HENNY acts out the fable in the
background.

FUTURE

Lonely at the top? That's to assume I wasn't lonely at the bottom.
This drive in me may be innate or it could just be a unique series
of events that led me to where I am now, but hear me when I tell
you that I begged—I begged them to come with me. But here I
stand alone.

PRESTON

I always knew there was more to life than waking up tired, to
work a job that'll pay you just enough to cover rent and a trip to
the LCBO on the weekend. That's how we're taught to live in this
country, as indentured slaves. Make a decent salary, 90% of which
disappears by Sunday afternoon, and the little you save on the side,
jump up inna carnival to celebrate surviving another year. Woi.

FUTURE

A couple of nights ago my wife was reading a bedtime story to
our baby girl, *The Little Red Hen*. I can't remember the last time I
heard it but it felt like, by the end, this was my autobiography laid
out in a children's book! You remember, the little red hen came
across some grain and saw it as a golden opportunity. She asked all
of the barn animals if they would help plant it, and every last one

of them replied: "I'm busy!" (I'm paraphrasing, this is the adult version.)

PRESTON
Who could I look up to for something different? A successful Black-owned business—that hires Black employees? No disrespect to my hair salons and restaurants but that's it? Where could I find a legacy like the ones I saw from every other foreigner settling into Canada, some of whom just got here the other day? In this country, I might as well be invisible because our businesses are here today and gone tomorrow, if at all. While other groups squeeze together to pool their resources, we're looking out for cheap. We'll bypass a brother selling fresh mangoes at the flea market because Walmart got them tuff rocks for sale.

FUTURE
So Ms. Henny said—

MS. HENNY
Aiight, I'll plant these seeds by my lonesome.

FUTURE
And the seeds grew into tall wheat stalks. Then she asked the barn animals if they would help cut the wheat and every last one of them replied: "I'm busy!"

PRESTON
Man, I've got family who've passed on their social housing unit from one generation to the next. That's not convenient, that's complacency. Social assistance is supposed to give you a hand up out of an unstable period, and should exist for that reason, but for us it has normalized poverty. Here's a simple shortcut to building

wealth: get a life-insurance policy. We seem to have money for everything but a casket. The inevitable. But what would our community look like if we could replace funeral fundraising with a down payment on a property? When I die, my assets will multiply.

FUTURE

The little red hen wore herself out cutting down the wheat and so badly wanted to rest. So she asked if anyone would share the load and help to grind it at the mill . . . and you know how every last one of them replied?

Points to the audience.

"I'm busy!"

PRESTON

I needed help, support, a break . . . more than people care to know. I started my business fifteen years ago with a vision, a vision that required painful sacrifices. My wife took on extra shifts to support our household so I could put my plans into action until finally my *first* sale! The rest is history. The business grew like anything, from nothing into something. Now the cash is rolling in and we're living comfortably, but it's the looks you get as a wealthy Black man, one who owns and manages an engineering firm that might as well translate to: "True, true, so what scams are you really finessing?"

FUTURE

The little red hen managed to grind all the wheat into flour and returned to the farm nearly burnt out. She asked if anyone would help her bake it, and you know how every last one of them replied?

Points to the audience.

"I'm busy!"

PRESTON
You know what people say to me now, looking at me as I stand today? "Hmph. You Mr. High Class. You don't know what it's like to be poor no more." And you know what, they're absolutely right. I started from the bottom just like you, but I always knew my worth.

FUTURE
Now the little red hen finally reached her moment of glory, with a perfectly baked, big, warm loaf of bread. She asked the crew, who'd like a slice of her laboured blood, sweat, and tears? And suddenly every last one of the animals piped up and said:

> *PRESTON joins in, impersonating a barn*
> *animal, all up in MS. HENNY's face.*

PRESTON
I'd be happy to take a slice or two or three off your wings, Ms. Henny.

FUTURE
And Ms. Henny said—

MS. HENNY
F-f-f-f-fuck y'all! I'm going to eat this whole loaf by my damn self.

SCENE 8

Exhibit A: Microaggressions in the workplace. LATRELL often daydreams of what it would be like to clapback at her co-worker like her life depended on it.

LATRELL

Note to self, don't listen to "Let's Get Free" before work.

Hell, I've been on edge ever since Rebecca took it upon herself to bawl out my name and say, "OMG. Latrell, is that your hair?" On sight. Like, I didn't even get to put my bag down good before she reached out for my tresses. Aht. Aht. I did a swift sidestep straight to my cubicle.

This is Rebecca who constantly reminds me that she has two biracial children that look like a cross between North West and Blue Ivy. But she "hates doing their hair." The same Rebecca who now believes I now have a moral obligation to officiate her into Blackness.

Rebecca thought wrong. I took a pregnant pause.

    Beat.

"What it look like, haux? Did I not just have some faux dreads last month and a 'Rihanna's crop' the month before?"

    Beat.

So I said, "Noooo, Rebecca, this is called a *weave."

    *Reference actor's actual hairstyle.

It allows me to be versatile, current, and ten times more fly than your boring ass blowout."

Beat.

ENSEMBLE *perform an* HBCU-*inspired choreographed step routine.*

So I said, "Girrrrrl, I thought you of all people could telllll . . . not-to-fuck-wit-me-todaaaaay. I just got four hours of sleep from submitting my grad school applicaSHUN, followed by a morning session with my man in between the sheeeeets. Then I prepped this vegan lunch for my new diet and realized I left my salted caramel chocolate on my dresser when you asked me that dumb ass question."

Beat.

So I said: nothing. I looked directly in her eyes and turned back to my computer and continued to do my job. She didn't bother to repeat herself, I'm positive she could read my mind.

SCENE 9

*Game show. This is an interactive part of
the play that requires the performers to be
attentive and improvise.*

HOST

Theme music.

Will your mom ever let you keep the change?
Is it canerows or cornrows?
Whose manz blew the OSAP bag on 'bana weekend?

Let's play a game of How Black Are You?!

End of theme music.

Let me let you in on a lil' secret: Black people are all the same.
Find out if you are Black enough to fit into our monolith. You
don't need to be Black to play, especially if you've been to Africa,
have at least one Black acquaintance, or listen to uncensored
urban music. For my Black folk who grew up in Barrie or as far
as Winnipeg, don't fret, you have just as much skin in the game as
someone from Rexdale.

I need three brave volunteers from our audience to unapologetically answer a few miscellaneous questions about "the culture."
The person who has the most correct answers wins.

*ENSEMBLE recruits volunteers from the
audience.*

Once volunteers are chosen, they sit side by side centre stage. The HOST asks them lighthearted introductory questions like their first name and where they're from. The questions may be changed or amended based on the community/city but should never come across as insulting or vulgar; avoid profanity, racial slurs, and trivia that is too niche to answer.

Contestants are given five seconds to answer.

Question #1: What Caribbean restaurant is most known for the saying "We nuh 'ave dat"?

Answer: Unfortunately, the soup, breakfast, or jerk chicken might be out at a Jamaican restaurant by the time your hungry belly arrives.

Question #2: Name the first Black prime minister of Canada?

Answer: Yes, that was a trick question. Prime Minister Justin Trudeau was caught black-handed sporting various painted-on ethnicities over the years. And because it's Canada, we apologized for him.

Question #3: Which supreme Goddess' birthday falls on September 4th?

Answer: Beyoncé. Beezus. Yoncé—are all acceptable answers.

Question #4: In what year did Caribana start?

Answer: 1967. Don't think your gran didn't catch a bubble and a wine before she was saved.

Question #5: At which Toronto intersection is the first and only Africentric Alternative School located?

Answer: Keele and Sheppard. Students start the day with a school-wide morning assembly reciting the Seven Principles of the Nguzo Saba and a daily affirmation. Bom, bom!

Bonus Question worth two extra points: Before Toronto was known as the 6ix, the city was dubbed T dot. Finish the words from the classic hit "BaKardi Slang" by Kardinal Offishall:

> *Ideally, a music clip of the actual song*
> *plays as a sound cue.*

Y'all think we all Jamaican, when nuff man are Trini's
Bajans, Grenadians and a hole heap of Haitians
Guyanese and all of the West Indies combined
To make the T dot O dot _____

Answer: One of a kind

Thank you for playing!

SCENE 10

*Growing up inna CanadeR.
The ENSEMBLE reminisces together, celebrating their youth. They flow through
personas (WEST INDIAN, GUYANESE,
GRANNY, JUVENILE, HOOD MAN). A
take on the "I AM CANADIAN" Molson
campaign. A beat is kept with hand
clapping and/or a cowbell.*

WEST INDIAN
i am ca-rib-bean
ackee, pone, bammy
rum punch, black cake
callaloo, breadfruit
doubles, fresh bake
provisions please
white rice or
rice n peas

GUYANESE
—um, no! peas-n-rice—

WEST INDIAN
riiiiiice-n-peeeeeas

    ENSEMBLE collective steups.

come, lewi start again.

i am carib-bean
steel pan melodies
mas camp ecstasy
corn soup outta van back
fete, j'ouvert
tek out yuh rag
bubble, wine, juk
jab jab
passa passa, bacchanal
bruk off yuh back!

GRANNY
shhhhhhh.
hush up.

WEST INDIAN
(whispers)
sunday service
shirt press, long dress
granny sey:

GRANNY
want a piece a candy?

WEST INDIAN
mint bribery
youth descent
loonie for a patty
in the church basement

(sighs)

ENSEMBLE
those were the days.

JUVENILE
summer bbq
dominos slapwey
cousins running n jumping
lovers rock thumpin n buzzing

ENSEMBLE
dj puuuuull up!

JUVENILE
jumbo freezies n sour keys
back then
you could ball
toonie tuesday
at sheridan mall

HOOD MAN
pssssst. my girl
call me after six on a weekday, eh?

ENSEMBLE
those were the days.
yup, those were the days.

SCENE 11

*If Marcus Garvey and Sister Souljah had
a daughter.*

*NO DISRESPEK enters with a large flip
chart and turns the first blank page over
to the next page that reads: Universal
Negro Improvement Association.*

NO DISRESPEK
Dear Black People,

Despite popular demand, this is the first and last time you will
hear me mention whyte people. The idolization of and sought out
approval from our former masters have cost us over 150 years of
liberation—post-emancipation—and as our viral sister so elo-
quently states, "Ain't nobody got time for that." As expected, since
I refuse to centre our colonizers, there goes 50% of my kinfolk.

Looks about the space as if watching people leave.

Peace be with you, Negroes.

Now with those of us remaining, with loose but intact mental
shackles living in Babylon, my message to you is this: are you
willing to die for your freedom? In the later 20th century, we have
been petted and purred with delight from advance integration
cheques. The promise to be treated as equal citizens in the Western
hemisphere so long as we work hard for someone outside of our
tribes and conform to worshiping the almighty dollar.

Integration is a sweet diabetes-filled dessert decorated in chocolate and vanilla swirls. Yummy. But my brothers and sisters, that tempting cake enclosed in a display glass is equivalent to the forbidden fruit in the Garden of Eden.

It's too late to refuse now, we've already gobbled down countless servings. How could you not be tempted when you've been used to eating literal waste: chicken foot, oxtail, souse, tripe. You think Black people are that into seasoning?

We need to break the cycle. It's time to rebuke the need to disrupt pale institutions that will only let one of us in at a time. Begging your oppressor for equity is as insane as whyte people leading whyte privilege workshops (oops, I said the "w" word, my bad).

Why protest for Blockorama funding despite it being THEE anticipated Pride event, whereas Anglo Saxon gay men click their ruby red heels and millions of dollars come glittering out of corporate-sponsored asses. Bank on that.

I know. Every time we manage to build something of our own, here comes the popo, the Canada Revenue Agency, or some claffy looking to sell us out. Did you ever stop to think that the ongoing wicked plots against our people are rooted in fear. That if we collectively stood our ground and protected what is ours, by any means necessary, Africa would be unstoppable. Wakanda is not our ceiling.

Meeting adjourned.

SCENE 12

*White Supremacist Patriarchal
Empowerment Conference.*

Leading up to his presentation, PETER
BRIDLEPATH *makes an epic entrance by
busting out a few signature dance moves.*

PETER BRIDLEPATH
Welcome to the meal ticket of the day: Diversity.

When you think of diversity, I want you to picture a rainbow with
a pot of gold at the end. The objective? To make minorities visible.

Reacts to sounds of discomfort in the crowd.

I know this approach may make some of us uncomfortable,
myself included, but I promise you that it's a means to a larger
end. Listen, slavery was the greatest, most profitable system the
Western world has ever produced. Granted it has slowed down
and inevitably become more expensive because, heck, we have to
pay these chimps—dollars and cents mind you. But now we have a
real chance here to profit off this "multiculturalism" thing.

All we have to do is hire more coloureds but we continue to hold
the power. Trust me, that will keep them singing hymns for at least
another century. Let's face it, we're getting smaller in numbers,
nobody wants to raise five brats, meanwhile these beasts are breeding
like crazy. Like I said, they just want to feeeeel represented. But here's
the brilliance, blacks, in particular, are our best asset and we love
them—as long as they stay in their place. Popular culture is nothing

without the blacks but they have no business acumen. Instead of copying their formula, why not have them give it to us directly. See, see? Now you're buying into it. Think of investing in their most promising trendsetters, that'll lead us to the cash cow quicker.

I'm telling you, I'm just so excited to be here today. We've got royalty in the house, people. You know who I'm talking about. It is my honour to introduce this dubious ruffian, the bad boy of imperialism! Ladies and gentlemen, welcome Derrick Harper.

DERRICK HARPER
Thank you, Pete. Give it up for Peter Bridlepath!

    Beat.

I want everyone to turn to Chapter 3 of your White Man Ally Manual.

    Beat.

Being a White Ally is a very lucrative position. Basically, you use your "white privilege." I didn't know "survival of the fittest" equalled privilege, am I right?

We need to push this diversity agenda, to get access without opposition to those underused, underdeveloped resources. Let's take Africville, prime land that could have made us a lot of money today. We used our old tried and true "houses to projects" pipeline but the darkies wouldn't budge. So we had to bulldoze it down, one by one, but it took so darn long that their resistance derailed our plan. Fast-forward, they have social housing and we have a dog park. Not a loss but far from a win.

We've got to continue to dangle the carrot, people. Repeat after me: bait and switch. They had land, infrastructure, careers, community. Put you're liberal hat on and sell some lies. "We can upgrade you from the dump to the promised land—a better, safer future for you and your family—just sign here." Then when the dust settles, they become renters, disorganized, unemployed, and in disagreement. Slowly blaming themselves, while we walk away scot-free.

We control the government, we control the media, we control the Goddamn world. Look at South Africa, kaffirs everywhere and we still have autonomy. How? Give one sellout power and he'll do the job better than you do. So don't worry about them tipping over the scale, it's safer to give them scraps than to starve the suckers. If they get too big, we'll just hire another black and feed them false information. Make it a competition, classic divide and conquer. Isn't that how we acquired Caribana. *(chuckles)*

Repeat after me: We'll take it from here.

SCENE 13

Presidential speech by WINNIE *continued.*

WINNIE
Haven't we seen history repeat itself time and time again, enough
to realize that this so-called democratic process will not benefit
any of the forty million South Africans subject to institution-
alized poverty and violence. How will a confession address the
85% of land seized by whites, who make up, what—15% of the
population?

I am calling for justice through reparations! I stand for a government that prioritizes the victims and not the perpetrators.
Apartheid is a rotten legacy of theft, dehumanization, torture,
murder, and constant fear, reigning over forty years. It is not
simply random acts of a few bad Dutch, German, English, and
French seeds but a system of oppression that has allowed for
people of sun-kissed skin, Africans, to be targeted and forced into
a calculated division of power.

SCENE 14

Grindin'. PRESTON *is finding out that it takes more than merit to climb the corporate ladder as one of the only two Black employees . . . it's more like Snakes & Ladders.*

PRESTON

I miss the ol' days when white people could and would speak
their mind
I'm tired of these white folk that hate niggers but offer you a cracker
The ones that parade their wokeness with every symbolic gesture
but can't even tell you and Bernard from marketing apart
And it's not just white folk, nowadays everybody got a blackcent
that they never seem to bring to the bank
Special shout out to the ones that ask, "Why do black people
always segregate themselves?" but never acknowledge that they do
the exact same thing
And don't get me started on the ones that make you go through
three callback interviews for an executive position just to hire
you for a junior role, with the same responsibilities and less pay.
But it's Fortune 500, so you accept and wait it out for six months
until your review comes up, because you've been smashing sales
records. And finally you get called on—

PETER BRIDLEPATH

Prezzy, my man! You've really been smashing records around
here—starting to make me look bad *(boisterous laugh)*. Here's the
thing, I know you know how to hook 'em but you haven't quite
mastered reeling 'em in.

PRESTON
Mr. Bridlepath, sir, I'm not following you. I haven't lost a single—

PETER BRIDLEPATH
Preston, Preston! It's nothing personal, man. Bringing in big accounts is one thing, but I can't afford for you to bite off more than you can chew and end up choking. These high-end clients have high-end expectations, if you know what I mean—

PRESTON
I don—

PETER BRIDLEPATH
So starting today, Brian—you know Brian, right? He'll be taking over those relationships. It's just protocol. However, I do have a colossal surprise for all your hard work. Tickets to tomorrow's game. My assistant went through hell to get these. They're not floor seats but it's the playoffs—GO Raptors!

SCENE 15

PASTOR
Frederick Douglass was born into slavery on a Maryland planta-
tion. Slavery was law. It was the supposed fate of Africans in the
Americas. Still, Frederick knew he was not born to be property of
another man. He said, "I prayed for twenty years but received no
answer until I prayed with my legs." "I prayed for twenty years but
received no answer until I prayed with my legs." How many of us
are praying without moving on our faith? The journey to freedom
is treacherous, but God will lead the way when you decide to
move. Stand up, pick up your mat, and walk!

Let me use a modern example. "First you over dedicate / then you
notice that you great / and you been the whole time / then it slap
you in the face." Y'all know the prophet Nipsey Hussle, right? First
you over dedicate—the lame man was stagnant for thirty-eight
years. That's not hard to believe, we see it every day. Nearly four
decades and nothing to show for his life. At that point he's past
the stage of crawling, he has to over dedicate and stand. "Then
you notice that you great / and you been the whole time / then it
slap you in the face." You ever been told you can't do something
that God put on your heart . . . and then you do. The man stood
and walked in the same instance, after thirty-eight years of being
stuck. Remember, faith without works is *(waits for congregation to
respond)* dead.

SCENE 16

HOTEP JIGGA *is third-eye woke and on a
mission to let light-skinned women know
that he's partial to ebony queens and has
no tolerance for colourism. But to quote
Kanye, "when he get on, he'll leave your
ass for a white girl."*

ANGELA *is catfished.*

HOTEP JIGGA

Responding to an ignorant comment:

Sorry hun, that mulatto coonery don't impress me
Thinking you're cuter than the brown skin sista
Cuz your skin a little lighter?
Fronting like you really like her but it's just competition
Double-dipping into your Black, then white gaze
I'll let you know straight, you don't get an automatic date
I ain't looking to have quote-unquote exotic yutes
That's not how my momma raised me
Now if you'll excuuuse me
There's a foine dark-skinneded hunny—high in fiber, iron, and fat
Maybe destined by fate
And she looks like she has more to offer than self-hate

ANGELA *enters.*

ANGELA
(to audience) You know what got me? So he asked me my name

and I said—

(to HOTEP JIGGA*)* Angela.

(to audience) And then he said—

HOTEP JIGGA
No, I want to know your African name, Empress.

ANGELA
(to audience) Like, I just died.

HOTEP JIGGA
My bad if I stepped to you with any negative vibrations, you don't deserve that, Queen.

(with a straight face) I want to build a vibe wit you
Connect and confide wit you
Truth is my third-eye sees through you
The God in me
Wants to enlighten you

ANGELA
(to audience) Is this jigga serious?!

(to HOTEP JIGGA*)* You really tryna rip off Common?

HOTEP JIGGA
Wooow. I feel crazy right now. I just want to impress you, still. I've never met a woman as beautiful and confident . . . you got me nervous. Listen, I genuinely want to build Black love. I need a strong Queen by my side. Let me prove it to you.

> ANGELA *and* HOTEP JIGGA *enact a short but intimate/heartfelt series of eight to ten tableaus that symbolize the relationship they've built over time. The final two tableaus insinuate that* HOTEP JIGGA *is drifting away and* ANGELA *is left confused. She draws him in one last time to seek closure.*

ANGELA
Black man. Ain't nobody finer than you
Ain't that what you tell me?
That our love is skin deep, pouring libations at my feet
Black man.
Yah, you walk it like you talk it. Mmm.
And got a big ol' rocket in your pocket
Black man.
And your love is like quicksand. Brother.
And you act brand new like no other
And you let my hand slip from your palm like butter
But you grip foreign with conviction
Hmm. That's real intres-ting.

It's deeper than complexion
And familiarity
It's deeper than trauma bonds
And ancestry.
When I see you, I see me.

Black love
      Legacy
            Fulfilled
                  Prophesy.

I don't know how to quit.
I wish I knew how to quit. Black man.
But you know what they say about
A strong Black woman.
She keeps going, and going, and going, and going
And holding, and showing, and growing, and sowing
For we.

The unseen sacrifice
I must have nine lives
And still died a thousand times
For you, Black man.
Left behind. Come to find babies that ain't mine.
Got the cold shoulder. Absorbed your deposited
Stress and washed the sheets with bleach.
Cooked with love and watched you eat. Black man.
Waited. And forgave. And then forgave me.

Got a house for myself and I live in peace.
See you sometimes, out my window,
Roaming the streets.
We say hi and bye, keep it short and sweet.
And I do what I gotta do
Oiled down and colourful,
Sunday brunch through obstacles
Laughing more than I cry.
You know why?

All of me deserves love.
Black woman.
I am that I am that I am
Enough.

SCENE 17

Chronicles of the tenement yahd.

FITZROY preaches to the masses.

FITZROY
fuck cyan compete wit bumbaclaat
bitch nuh live inna my vocabulary

nigger, is too choppy choppy
bredrin, miss me with dat
no sah, yuh cyan compete wit

> *ANGELA enters the scene and walks in front of FITZROY,*
> *minding her own business.*

(to ANGELA) yuh look like a sweet tin ah condense milk.

ANGELA
Excuse me?

FITZROY
mi wan put a likkle hard dough bread inna yuh cornmeal
porridge.

ANGELA
Did you not just watch the last scene?

> *ANGELA kisses teeth.*

> *ANGELA exits the scene.*

FITZROY

(brushes off rejection) see how we season up we dialect?
bumbaclaat rossclaat pussyclaat
dat last one too raw, nuh tru?
yuh nuh muss have feelin inna yuh talk, nuh tru?
itz all vibrashuns, nuh tru?

> *FITZROY improvs street interaction between two friends for a few beats.*

"whaampm star?"

(daps) "mi dey yah my yout"

> *Improv ends.*

(to audience) simple tings, from de greetin to de feelin
good mawnin, good evelin
uncle, aunty, broddah, mumma, puppa
ah so yuh mus greet people
simple tings

den we gah school
education
indoctrination
socialization
yuh mean dem give yuh head ah good brainwashin
now yuh nah nuh sense come talk bout
terminology in psychology
compartmentalized meanings
kleptomaniac.
ah wha dat? you mean tief she ah tief!

psycho induced coma.
nuh maad 'im maad?
'ole'ep ah choppy choppy tings fi cloud up unnu mind

dem ah stifle dem talk
dem ah stifle dem walk
squeeze up dem batty so
scowl and scoff
jah rastafari! i n i nuh rate dat
di riddim dey inna my blood
mi kiss teet like mi stomp feet
(kisses teeth)
but yuh nuh ready fi dis yet

SCENE 18

BLACK TWITTER

I'm sorry, but am I the only one looking at these land acknowledgments sideways?

So we're calling out the umpteem names of First Nations people but still celebrating Thanksgiving? We're acknowledging the traditional and ancestral lands upon which we gather but still poisoning the land and water that communities are fighting to protect? We're still acting like this is a "we" problem when we all know that it's a "you" problem. Take full responsibility with your hudsons-bay-smallpox-carrying-animal-extinction-residential-school-aparthied-tactic-lookin-ass.

SCENE 19

It is April 1851. We are inside the St. Lawrence Hall in Toronto where FREDERICK Douglass has been invited as a guest lecturer by the Anti-Slavery Society of Canada.

FREDERICK finds himself unusually uncomfortable.

FREDERICK
Friends and Fellow Citizens . . . Members of the Society . . .

FREDERICK turns away from the podium and faces the actual audience in a stream of consciousness.

I have delivered many a speech. At great length. From my first place of refuge, Lynn, Massachusetts, to the muggy streets of Paisley, Scotland. When I was invited to speak by the Anti-Slavery Society of Canada I immediately accepted, as I had a wild curiosity to see, for myself, where tens of thousands of my people have escaped horror and found refuge, in a not-so-distant land. I was paid handsomely, the smoothest of transactions, effortless.

Beat.

Nevertheless, I have seen little evidence of a promised land—why would this country have such a society with not so much as a Negro in sight? It is such a violent sensation to drown in whiteness and firm handshakes. To see men salivate as I speak, tickled by my eloquence. To be considered a marvel of beasts. Although I speak for the oppressed, my abolitionist work has been perverted. For my father's blood, the colonization of my anatomy, is deemed the logical credit of my brilliance. Is this skin that clothes my soul merely a vessel for another man's desires?

As I stand in this chamber for local city council, I am washed in an unexpected terror that silently reins my body hostage. These men, passively affluent, anchor at the forefront—peacocking their privilege. I am accustomed to grimace, densely threaded hoods, weapons carried openly . . . and now I stand surrounded in a packed room. A few brothers are among the crowd but not with the crowd. I can see it in their eyes, that they do not have to run anymore, but they too are surrounded. Standing in this room, it has struck me that these Canadian men believe themselves to be good. Stainless. I can sniff scents of slavery, even in this new construction . . . but there are no signs of the source. This is no haven for my people, merely a surveilled resting place. I never thought this yearning would ever come in my lifetime, but I cannot wait to return back home.

SCENE 20

*An old man and young man reason about
the state of the ghetto mentality.*

OLD HEAD
Before, we tore the flesh off our brothers back for claps from the
master
Got so used to killing each other we "6ixBuzz" that shit
Slap and kick unwanted memories out one another
Drag and butcher
And pop off on any pussy
That want some
Yea son, we bred like dat
Conditioned to hate our own image
God's children who were called little devils
So keep your eyes straight when you walk past my gate

REAL TALK
Crazy, we still calling each other niggas
Reclaiming my ass
We know the origins, fact is fact
When a cop kills one of us he's a punk ass bitch

OLD HEAD
But when the gangbanger missed and shot that little girl—

REAL TALK
—ain't nobody snitch
Crazy, we still claiming the hood
It's not all bad, but it ain't all good
Four kids in an apartment and daddy can't be on the lease

Daddy can't make enough 9–5, so daddy in the streets
Crazy, we still don't love these hoes
She been around the block and everybody knows
She's been held down by Unc and anything goes
She said yes to the train but you know she meant no
Crazy, we don't even know the half of where we come from

OLD HEAD
And them white people right, we don't like the cold

REAL TALK
Facts. We make the best of the least
Sometimes just surviving to eat
Man, I have yet to live free
To worry about silly bullshit and kick up my feet
Maybe love my girl like she love me

OLD HEAD
Facts. But we still here
Change don't come overnight
Remember someone gave up their life
So you wouldn't have to fight
Give it time, young blood
Take it from me
We chose to have knowledge, to see what God sees

SCENE 21

BLACK TWITTER

There's nothing sweeter than the sound of white noise. White noise occurs when an unsuspecting white person tries to undermine the intelligence of a person of colour only to be verbally whipped and slayed through facts and wit leaving their opponent stricken, speechless, and a face flushed with blood.

SCENE 22

My brother's keeper.

WITNESS retells his account of seeing 23's interaction with the police after being pulled over in the hood.

Performer playing WITNESS and 23 goes back and forth between portraying both characters.

Performer playing WHITE COP and BLACK COP goes back and forth between portraying both characters.

WITNESS

Recounts the incident.

They said he was resisting arrest. That's just code for asking questions.

WHITE COP

Takes a great deal of time to circle 23's car with a flashlight before approaching the driver's window.

Licence and registration.

23
Why am I being stopped?

WHITE COP
I saw you were parked here for a while. Just making sure everything is okay.

23
I'm good.

Gives WHITE COP *his licence and registration.*

WHITE COP
(admiring car) This is a very nice ride.

Where'd you get it?

23
(annoyed) The dealership.

WHITE COP
All by yourself? *(flashing light)* And these clothes and shoes in the back? You've got some receipts on you? You do know this is a large amount of merchandise.

Any guns or drugs in the car?

23
Why? Cause I'm a young Black man?

(boastful) I don't need a gun to get what I want.

WHITE COP
(challenged) Excuse me?

23

The service not paying you enough to buy Jordans? It's only $300, Bro. I can spot you and you don't even gotta to pay me back, it just wouldn't feel right.

WHITE COP
Step out of the car.

23
For what?

WHITE COP
(to dispatch radio) I'm going to need backup.

WITNESS

Resumes narrating the scene.

I watched as five police officers slammed their batons from the top of his head to the soles of his feet. Two with their boots on the back of his head. I stood watching guard, told myself I was making sure they didn't violate him, or worse, but all I could see was myself.

My legs, my whole body was stiff, seized by fear. My heart was beating like I was about to die. I was scared. Too scared to act, cause if I was to jump in and try and save him they might kill us both, bring in two more squad cars, just so they could take turns, have a pignic. We're already in the hood, the perfect territory to be invisible.

And there was that one Black officer with his heart beating like mine. His colleague took notice of his lack of force saying, "What, you feel sorry for this punk? These low-lifes have no fucking respect, you have to show them what the law feels like." I knew he was feeling the same way as me, knowing, 'The only thing saving me is this uniform, but it don't erase this Black skin.'

That's what he's thinking as he raises his stick to my brother, beating him harder than every other officer.

BLACK COP acts out the beating.

Hoping he dies because at least there'll be no more pain. That's fucked up, right?

NO DISRESPEK enters discreetly.

I couldn't even record it. It would've just been evidence that I didn't do something when he needed me, that I was just a bystander to his murder. My brother . . .

NO DISRESPEK shoots BLACK COP.

> *Time and space are disrupted with the unexpected introduction of an alternate ending that does not fit in with the reality the characters can wrap their heads around.*

WITNESS / BLACK COP

> *Both lines overlap.*

You can do that?! /

> / You can't do that!

NO DISRESPEK
Really? So what, I was just supposed to let him *(refers to* BLACK COP*)* beat the kid to death. Not on my watch.

WITNESS
But why shoot the Black cop, tho?

NO DISRESPEK
He chose a side.

SCENE 23

Presidential speech by WINNIE *continued.*

WINNIE

For my first command as president, I will order the deportation of all Afrikaners and respective whites back to their original home-lands, along with repossession of all current property and raw resources owned by the outgoing apartheid government. Power and resources will be redistributed to the rightful South Africans. Spare us the half-truths of a Boer therapy session. We know exactly what happened and it is time to finally address the cause of the sickness. For anyone who believes this is a harsh command, I ask you to remember the countless strategies the Afrikaners have inflicted upon us, such as the Group Areas Act and the Black Communities Development Act where we were ripped from our homes, our land, sorted by tribes, dumped in the middle of nowhere, had our citizenship revoked, and our opportunities flattened.

Let our suffering not be in vain and trivialized with a band-aid solution. We need proper healing to rebuild our nation. Unlike our brothers and sisters scattered across the world, tangled in the same corrupt racist systems we face—South Africans, we are the majority! Let us not miss this moment to reclaim our future!

SCENE 24

Church, we have a sister in here running. Sister Brown is running for city council, and based on her character, experience, and platform, everyone should be supporting her campaign—especially for the benefit of our own community. But you know, the lame excuse is we don't involve ourselves in politics—only complain about being counted out. We have two brothers, Zayden and Nassir, running a free after-school program for the past two years. The gym at the community centre is not extending their space agreement and they currently can't find a replacement. I know we have someone in the church with a connection, and hosting a fundraiser would guarantee at least another two years of financing for these incredible youth investing in youth. And let's not forget Sister Pearly, seventy-odd years young, and every weekend she's out providing food and care packages to the homeless. If you know what it's like to be hungry or down on your luck—then you have an obligation to help those less fortunate.

All these runners would be able to have a greater impact if we all stood up, picked up our mat, and walked. It's not merely enough to provide for your own needs, we, as a church, need to make movement fundamental to our mission. Starting this week, an hour of service—an hour, not an extra hour, Sister Pearly—will be dedicated to canvassing, volunteering, donating, mentoring—whatever our community needs to make it whole—to uplift God's people.

Disciples, if we're not over-dedicating, moving on our faith, then we'll be in the same place thirty-eight years from now, justifying our hopeless state with the injustices of the world. Do we want to be whole? I said do WE want to be whole? I need somebody in here today to stand up! Pick up your mat! And WALK!

SCENE 25

The following text is meant to be delivered as voices in a Black person's head of stereotypes that surface on a day-to-day basis. STICKS N STONES, played by the other two performers, circle around PRESTON, taunting him with each word.

PRESTON

He starts to obsess about what his boss just said (revealed in Scene 25.2).

What did he mean by that?

STICKS N STONES slither in with the intention of breaking PRESTON's spirit.

They speak triggering words and phrases one after the other.

STICKS N STONES
the absent black father /
deadbeat daddy /
baby momma /
at-risk /
promiscuous /
hide yo kids /
hide yo wife /
female genital mutilation /
gangstas /

thugs /
criminals /
the angry black woman /
hutu /
tutsi /
underprivileged /
illiterate /
dropouts /
incarcerated /
bad bitch /
black on black crime /
priority neighbourhoods /
neighbourhood improvement area /
you the real MVP /
most vulnerable people.

The pace speeds up.

aids/hiv /
poverty /
ebola /
save a child for just a dollar a day /
uncivilized /
primitive /
third world /
underdeveloped /
oh my god, look at her butt /
dark skin /
light skin /
nigga nigga nigga /
inherently violent /
dysfunctional /

chicken head /
diabetes /
i'm lovin' it /
adhd /
welfare /
gold chains /
civil war /
what's wrong with you people? /
the suspect is a black male last seen wearing a hoodie found
shots
shots
shots
shots
shots
shots—

PRESTON

Breaks scene.

Dead! I get it! I'm sorry, I'm trying to keep up the pace with this
show but y'all know it's draining as fuk to be talking about race all
the damn time. Like allll the time. Can we please take a moment of
silence to just be?

Moment of silence is held by ENSEMBLE.

SCENE 25.2

PRESTON

Thank you. I appreciate that cause I be needing a break. Damn. In the "Great White North" you really have to be checking yourself about every little microaggression.

> *Beat.*

Today, in front of everyone in the office, my boss says to me, "Preston, I know you have your ears to the street. What's minimum wage?"

SISTREN / BREDRIN

Oh, shit!
Oh, hell naw!
For real?

PRESTON

Right?! What the fuck do I know about minimum wage? I'm the top sales rep breaking six figures in commission. You, know what I told him?

SISTREN / BREDRIN

Watchu tell em?

PRESTON

You really wanna know what I told him?

SISTREN / BREDRIN

Watchu tell em, dogg?

PRESTON
(dramatic) "Google it, nigga."

Blackout.

SCENE 25.3

The group unwinds in laughter together in the dark. House lights gradually come up.

BREDRIN

Yoooooo, the man said, "Google it, nigga!" I'm dead!

SISTREN

So, Preston, where are you working tomorrow?

PRESTON

Don't watch dat.

BREDRIN

No, for real though because when you took me to the playoffs game with you, I wanted to give in my resume. I mean I never been so close to the court. I could see the sweat drippin' off niggas.

PRESTON

Look, I'm not pressed for the job. I'm definitely not pressed for basketball tickets. Believe me. I'm just tired of getting underhanded.

SISTREN

Whatever happened to your plans for launching your own engineering firm? You've been bringing in clients, why not use this opportunity to start now?

Beat.

PRESTON

You're so right. The longer I work for these companies, the richer I make them. It's going to take a while to get a new firm on its feet but I know I've got enough skills, knowledge, and contacts to compete with the best of them.

Beat.

Honestly, I'd love for you both to be a part of it.

(to SISTREN) You know how to manage operations in and out.

(to BREDRIN) And you can handle manufacturing.

(to both SISTREN and BREDRIN) I'll focus on generating venture capital and development but you'll each get shares in the firm that'll mature and be worth your investment over time. What do you say?

SISTREN & BREDRIN

Both look at each other and then at PRESTON.

I'm busy.

The end.

ACKNOWLEDGEMENTS

This play is a tribute to Toronto, a fragmented offering of hip-hop, church, Black love, politics, identity, sorrow, joy, rebellion, and, and, and.

To my parents, Cora and Brian, I'm still trying to wrap my head around what you've sacrificed to make our lives so easy breezy. To my siblings, Tinesha, Brianna, Zion, and River, I can't imagine life without you. To my mentors and guides, ahdri zhina mandiela, d'bi.young anitafrika, Philip Akin, Meredith Potter, Vivine Scarlett, Weyni Mengesha, and Dr. Deloris Seiveright, I treasure your selfless leadership. To my OG cast, Dennis Langley, David Delisca, and Angaer Arop, we manifested two of the most magical years filled with memories I will cherish foreverrr. To my TPM cast, Chris Parker, Uche Ama, and Chris Bautista, you understood the assignment! To my producer, Troy Defour, through thick and thin you've never left my side, and for that—you can't get rid of me!

To my dawta, Mulu-Reign, for staying put during rehearsals and being more dramatic than me xoxo. And to Patrick for selling a hundred copies in advance because you are my number one fan. Thank you to Andy McKim for saying yes, Marjorie Chan, Regine Cadet, and every Theatre Passe Muraille staff that supported the premiere. Much love to Donna-Michelle St. Bernard and Lincoln Anthony Blades for your dramaturgical guidance. Special thank you to Black Theatre Network, Laura Nanni and the SummerWorks

Festival, Toni Simmons Henson and the Atlanta Black Theatre Festival, Hélène Mateev and Théâtre de l'Usine, Halifax Fringe, and the DC Black Theatre & Arts Festival for programming the play. Thank you to the Canada Council for the Arts, Ontario Arts Council, and Toronto Arts Council for your generous funding, as well as the Consulate General of Canada in Atlanta for a warm welcome. I am so grateful for the collaborative publishing process—a special thank you to Annie Gibson, Blake Sproule, Jessica Lewis, and Avvai Ketheeswaran at Playwrights Canada Press!

To Yvonne Su for pushing my work and Levi Lingwabo for our fateful conversation where I blurted out the title of this play.

Last but not least, this would be all for naught without the people aka audience. Thank you for showing up, showing out, asking questions, challenging what you witnessed, spreading the word, coming back, hugs, laughing out loud, and revelling in the liveness of theatre.

Natasha Adiyana Morris is a soft-spoken, dramatic storyteller. Born in Winnipeg and raised in Toronto's West End—in the most encouraging and full'up Jamaican household—being (h)extra is in her blood. Recognized for founding PIECE OF MINE Arts, an initiative that presents works in progress by Black play creators, she owes a great deal to the esteemed tutelage of b current, anitafrika! dub theatre, Obsidian Theatre, and Volcano Theatre. Her debut production *The Negroes Are Congregating* (PIECE OF MINE Arts, Theatre Passe Muraille) was nominated for a Dora Mavor Moore Award for Outstanding New Play. She is honoured to be a Soulpepper Academy and York University (Sociology B.A.) alumni.